The Indo-Pacific Library

INDONESIA

Graham Houghton & Julia Wakefield

CONTENTS

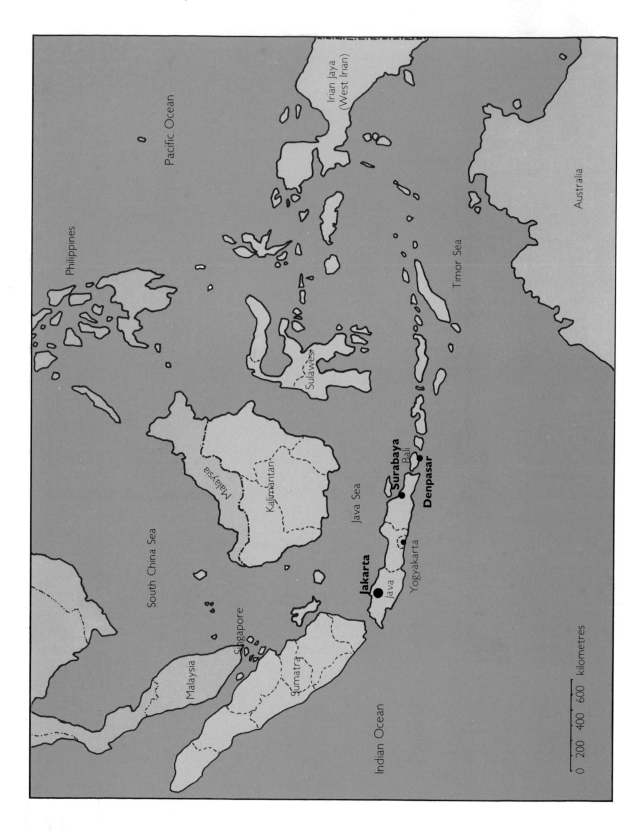

Geography

The Land

Indonesia is made up of five main islands and over 13 000 smaller ones. It is the largest group of islands in the world. Most of the islands were formed by volcanic activity and there are still about 100 active volcanoes in Indonesia today. Indonesia has many high mountains which are covered by thick tropical rainforests. The highest mountains are in Irian Jaya and they often exceed 4000 metres in height. Although Indonesia is on the Equator these mountains often have a permanent snow cover, because of their great height.

Rivers and Lakes

There are few rivers of any size but the waters from the many streams and lakes which form in the craters of old volcanoes are often used to irrigate crops.

The sea around most of the major islands is never more than about 220 metres deep. But between the Island of Kalimantan and Irian Jaya to the east, the sea can be up to 4500 metres deep.

Climate

Because Indonesia lies along the Equator, it has what is known as a tropical monsoon climate. This means that it has a wet and dry season. The dry season lasts from May to October and the rainy season lasts from November to April, although heavy rains can and do fall at all times of the year.

The temperature changes little during the year, but does vary between highland (cooler) and lowland (hotter). The humidity is usually high and this can make it feel hotter near the coast than inland.

Tea is grown on large estates which employ local villagers

Plants and Animals

Indonesia can be divided into two parts when we look at the native plants and animals to be found there. In the western islands such as Sumatra, Java, Bali, and Kalimantan the types of plants and animals are the same as those found on the South East Asian mainland. The animals include tigers, elephants, the rare one-horn rhinoceros, deer, monkeys, wild boar and the orang utan. Among the trees which grow in the western islands are teak and meranti; both provide wood for builders and for furniture makers.

The animals of the eastern islands are more closely related to those found in Australia, for example, the cassowary, the cockatoo, the tree kangaroo and the red koala. These islands were once joined to Australia many thousands of years ago. One of the most famous of all Indonesian animals is the Komodo Dragon. Like the Australian goanna the Komodo Dragon is a monitor lizard. It is found only on the island of Komodo and can grow to a length of two metres or more.

History

Ancient History

During Indonesia's long history, people from many different places have moved into the various islands. They were attracted by the fertile soils for farming and by the natural products such as spices and timber of the region. But Indonesia was inhabited long before the farmers arrived and some very important finds of the remains of early man over half a million years old have been discovered there.

People

The original inhabitants of Indonesia came from Malaysia and as far away as China. They arrived at a time when some of the islands were joined to the mainland by dry land. These people probably lived in small villages and grew various crops including rice. They were also good sailors and traded across the Indian and Pacific Oceans. Contacts made through this trade brought other settlers from India and Arabia.

Europeans in Indonesia

The first European known to have visited Sumatra and Java was Marco Polo in 1292. In 1511 Portuguese traders arrived in search of spices and they were quickly followed by the Spanish. The Dutch too were interested in Indonesia and by the early seventeenth century the Dutch East India Company had taken control of the spice and coffee trade. They also established themselves as the colonial rulers of Indonesia with their headquarters in Batavia, now called Jakarta, but this rule was very unpopular.

The Napoleonic Wars

During a period of wars in Europe when Holland was occupied by the forces of France under the Emperor Napoleon, the British East India Company took control of Indonesia from 1811 to 1816. The Governor at this time was Sir Thomas Stamford Raffles who went on to establish Singapore in 1819. Raffles introduced a certain amount of self-government and stopped the local slave trade. After Napoleon was defeated by the British at the Battle of Waterloo, the Dutch returned to Indonesia and were only forced to leave again by the Japanese in 1942. Between 1816 and 1942 there were many rebellions against Dutch rule in Indonesia.

Independence

At the end of the Second World War in 1945, Indonesia declared itself to be a free, independent nation, and in 1949 Indonesia officially became Independent. But it was not until 1956 that the Dutch finally left the islands.

The Capital

The capital of Indonesia is Jakarta. The city was given this name in 1527 to celebrate a victory against the Portuguese who had tried to conquer it. Jakarta means 'City of Victory'.

Jakarta is a modern city with international architecture

The Government

Indonesia is a sovereign, independent republic. The President (currently General Suharto) is the head of State. Indonesia declared itself an independent state in 1945, and officially became so in 1949. Ahmed Sukarno (1901–1970) was appointed President. In 1963, Sukarno was elected President for life by the Parliament. An attempted coup in 1965 put Sukarno in an embarrassing situation because he was thought to be behind the coup with the Communists, but the Military could not substantiate their claims. In 1966, Suharto and the Military took over the executive power of the State leaving Sukarno as President. In 1967 Sukarno handed over all his power to Suharto. In 1968, Suharto was elected president by the Parliament and was re-elected in 1973, 1978 and 1983. He currently holds the posts of Prime Minister and Minister of Defence.
Since the declaration of independence there has been a general election (i.e. for the people) in 1955, and one every five years since 1969. General elections are held for parliament; parliament elects the President.

Indonesia's House of Representatives

Natural Resources

Indonesia is rich in most of the important natural resources. The combination of high mountain ranges and high rainfall means that dams can be built to provide hydro-electricity for both industry and homes. There are also several power stations which use locally mined coal and natural gas.

Oil

Indonesia is the largest producer of oil in South East Asia and exports much of its produce to other refineries such as those in Singapore.

Mineral Mining

Most of the major mining projects are to be found on the island of Java. However, copper is mined in Irian Jaya and nickel is produced on Sulawesi. Indonesia is one of the world's largest producers of tin, most of which is exported. Bauxite for the production of aluminium is another important mineral. Iron ore, silver and gold are also mined.

Rice grown on terraces such as these is an important basic food crop

Life in the Country

Agriculture in Indonesia is a mixture of traditional and modern methods and machinery.

The Rice Crop

As in many of the other countries in the region, rice is the most important crop. Two or even three crops can be grown each year in areas where there is plenty of water. The canals and ditches which carry the water to the rice fields are often used for fish farming and breeding ducks. At harvest time everybody, young and old alike, lends a hand. The rice crop is usually cleaned and prepared in the village ready to be taken to market.

Markets

Many locally produced items can be bought in the village markets. Apart from food items there may be pots, basketwork and straw hats, musical instruments and farming needs such as bullock-ploughs and spare parts for small machines.

A wide range of goods can be bought in the markets

Increases in the production of three vital foodstuffs. The figures stand for thousand tonnes

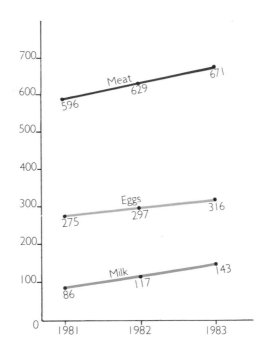

Social Life

Village life is usually well-organised with an elected council looking after the needs of the people. Every so often a touring theatre group might give a performance of a play and there are often other entertainments such as a village dance. Sports are encouraged and neighbouring villages might play each other at football or basketball.

If there is a river or stream near the village it often becomes an important meeting place as people gather to wash clothes, to fish or just to go for a swim.

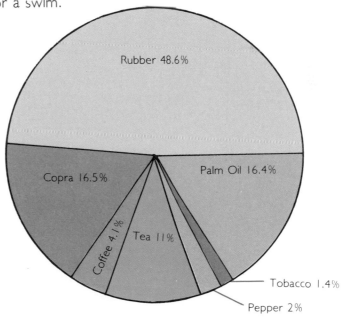

Crops exported as a percentage of the total

Rubber is an important export crop

Crops for Export

Many of the crops grown are for overseas markets. These crops include coffee, rubber, tea, tobacco, palm products such as oil and copra, timber and spices. They are grown on larger farms and estates which employ local villagers to look after the crops and harvest them when they are ready.

Livestock Farming

Cattle and buffaloes are raised not only for meat and milk, but also for transporting goods to market and for work in the fields such as ploughing. Chickens are kept for their meat and eggs and sheep, goats and pigs are also important food animals.

There are some very unusual and specialised farms in parts of Indonesia. In Irian Jaya, for example, crocodiles are farmed for the leather made from their skins.

Industry and Commerce

Indonesia has many modern industries that obtain their raw materials locally. For instance, the tyre makers have a ready supply of rubber, and the plastic and chemical industries can rely on Indonesia's own oil production for the goods that they need.

Two of the most important products of the chemical industry are fertilisers and insecticides for farm use. Other industries support Indonesian agriculture by producing factory and farm machinery. Glass and explosives are also produced locally in large quantities.

Factories

The engineering industry produces a wide range of goods both for home and overseas. There is a well-developed car industry as well as important shipyards at Jakarta and a number of aircraft factories. Paper is made on a large scale. Textile factories produce up to 1.5 billion metres of cloth each year although much of the raw material for this industry needs to be imported, for example, wool from Australia and cotton from China.

Small Industry

Indonesia is keen to help its smaller industries, and many small-scale industrial estates have been built to provide workshop facilities for them. Woodcarving is one such industry which is based on skill and long training rather than mass production. The production of decorative silverware, or fine basketry are other examples. Indonesian crafts are usually displayed at many of the major trade fairs held in various parts of the world.

This modern factory in west Java produces both civil and military aircraft

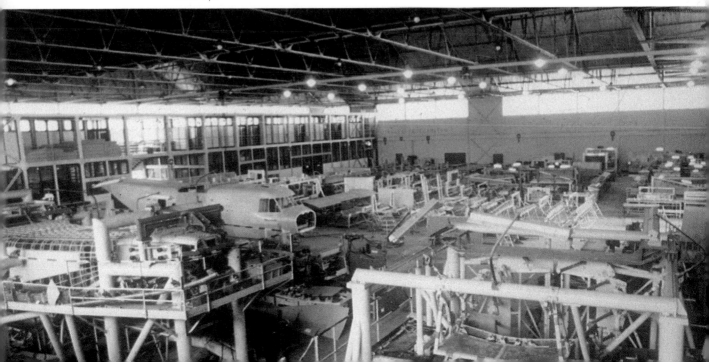

Transport and Communication

Indonesia stretches for about 5152 kilometres from east to west and needs an efficient transport system to keep all its 13 500 islands in contact with each other. Ships and planes are both very important.

Shipping

The Indonesians have always had a fine reputation as seafarers and even up to the year 1900, still visited the northern coast of Australia to collect *trepang*, or sea cucumber, which is a favourite food particularly in China. These voyages were made in ships called *prahus* (pronounced prows). Prows are still made in Sulawesi to a design which is hundreds of years old and they are very seaworthy.

Bulk goods such as iron ore are carried between the islands in ships. Many of the islands do not have an airstrip and they rely entirely on these ships for supplies of essentials such as food, clothing and equipment.

Indonesia's own merchant shipping line (PELNI) carries much of the goods that are exported and imported to and from other countries.

Prahus built in Sulawesi are still used for the transport of goods over thousands of kilometres of ocean

Air Transport	Aircraft are used to transport both people and goods to the remoter parts of the larger islands as well as between islands. Airstrips are often built high in the mountains to serve a new industrial development such as a mine and these flights are called 'Pioneer Flights'. In the past people would only be able to reach these areas after a long slow overland journey over poor roads through thick rainforests. Aircraft are used to transfer sick or injured people to centres where there are major hospitals.
Roads	Many of the traditional means of transport are still in use in the remote areas. These include horses, bullock carts and even human carriers. But even in the remote areas trucks, buses and motor cars are the most important means of transporting goods and people today.
Railways	The islands of Java and Sumatra both have good railway systems which were begun by the Dutch. Goods carried on the railways include cement, fertilisers, coal, iron and steel, and oil.

The railways in Sumatra carry goods to communities that might otherwise be very isolated

Life in the Cities

Modern cities in Indonesia are similar to those found anywhere in the world. Multi-storey office blocks and modern shops line the streets. At night there is much to do with plenty of cinemas and other entertainments.

It is still possible to travel in a pedal-powered *becak* or three-wheeled taxi, but these are giving way to motorised taxis called *bemos*.

Markets and shopping centres in the cities are usually clean and spacious places in which to shop and offer a full range of goods for sale. There are still the street vendors, however, who usually sell small souvenirs and trinkets.

There are many private cars in Indonesia

Population

Indonesia has the fifth largest population in the world, with the majority of people living on the island of Java. Indonesians have learned to be very tolerant of different groups within society. The people of Irian Jaya, for instance, have a very different way of life from those in Java. To complicate matters further there are about 250 different languages and dialects spoken throughout Indonesia. Although there is an official Indonesian language which is based on Malay, the government encourages the preservation of the local minority languages. This means that many Indonesians speak more than one language.

Bali has many colourful ceremonies based on Hindu traditions

Religion

The people of Indonesia are free to practise any religion that they choose. However, the main religion is Islam which was first brought to the islands by Arab traders. Christianity, Hinduism, and Buddhism all exist in Indonesia and there are certain areas where most people will follow one of these. On Bali, for example, Hinduism is the most popular religion.

The Grand Cathedral in Jakarta is a centre for Indonesian Christians

Education

Every young person in Indonesia is entitled to receive an education. Below the age of 7 a child may go to kindergarten and then a pre-primary school. Between the ages of 7 and 12 children attend primary school. The primary schools are generally run by the government and most of them give an education based on Islamic traditions. There are also various private schools.

Secondary Education

In high school one of the most important subjects is science, but art, maths and sport are all part of the daily timetable. English is the first foreign language taught in most schools.

Traditional Music and Dance

It is considered important in Indonesia that children learn the traditional music and dances of their region. In Bali it is said that a child learns to dance while it is still a babe in arms. Strict formal training in the dances associated with Bali's many festivals begins at about 6 years of age.

Education is the right of all Indonesian children

Health and Welfare

Besides the usual health care facilities such as clinics and hospitals, much time and money is spent on stopping outbreaks of disease. A supply of clean drinking water to all parts of the country is one of the aims of the government. There are also efforts to improve the food that people eat. There are many public education drives to tell people how to prevent the spread of diseases such as malaria and about the dangers of drug abuse.

Hospitals in the major cities are up to date and can provide most modern surgical needs.

Indonesia is always improving its roads and bridges. Structures such as this will soon disappear

Architecture

Traditional architecture styles vary widely throughout the Indonesian islands. Wood is the most common building material outside the cities, although bamboo is often used too. The traditional roofing material is thatch, but nowadays corrugated iron is commonly used. In areas of marshy and swampy ground and near the coast, houses are raised on stilts. Houses are often highly decorated and have a very distinctive shape to the roofs.

The Buddhist temple at Borobudur was partially restored by Sir Stamford Raffles

Arts and Crafts

The best known craft product of Indonesia is batik. This is cloth which has been treated and dyed in a special way so as to produce an intricate pattern. Real batik is produced in Java, but batik designs are printed on to cloth in other parts of Indonesia. Weaving, using a variety of yarns such as cotton, wool and silk is another traditional skill throughout the region. The stone and wood carvings of Indonesia are world famous as is the silverwork which is produced on a number of islands.

The Hindu temples of Indonesia are highly decorated with traditional stone carvings

Opposite: Traditional Indonesian buildings have very distinctive roof lines

Festivals and Ceremonies

Art and religion are often difficult to separate from each other in Indonesia. Each of the four main religions has its own celebrations. The Muslims fast during the daylight hours for a month during Ramadan and the Christians observe Easter and Christmas as well as a number of Saints' days.

Indonesian puppets

The island with more festivals than any other is Bali. Here as in the rest of Indonesia the performance of the *Wayang*, a type of theatre which uses live actors or puppets, is not just entertainment, but also a serious ritual. There are two forms of puppet theatre, the *Wayang Golek* which uses ordinary puppets made of wood and the *Wayang Kulit* which uses flat puppets made of leather. The puppet operator or *Dalang* is looked upon as a priest, and his costume and the puppets themselves are often thought of as sacred emblems. The performances of the *Wayang* are often based on old Hindu legends. The *Gamelan* Orchestra accompanies performances of *Wayang*. The *Gamelan* is made up of string instruments similar to violins and zithers, and also of percussion instruments such as the drum-like *bonangs* and xylophones or *Gambang*. Most of the instruments are made of metal and there may be more than seventy of them in a *Gamelan* Orchestra.

A Gamelan Orchestra

There are many other festivals most of which involve months of preparation and may use costly decorations and offerings which are destroyed at the end of the ceremony. Funeral ceremonies on Bali are usually colourful, noisy affairs.

Harvest time is also a time of celebration and thanksgiving for the crops gathered in. Offerings of food are made in temples and churches as well as on family altars.

Some of the instruments of the Gamelan Orchestra

A funeral ceremony in Sulawesi involves the whole community

Sport and Recreation

National Sport Day The first national games in Indonesia took place in September 1948. As a result, 9 September each year is now the national sports day.

National Competition Indonesian sportsmen and women have won many international competitions in games such as badminton, football and basketball.

Independence Day Celebrations As part of Indonesia's independence day celebrations, colourful canoe races are held in southern Sumatra. Each canoe has twenty people paddling it.

Bull Racing Perhaps the most spectacular event is the bull-racing which takes place on the island of Madura off the coast of Java. These races are said to have begun as ploughing matches between farmers. A rider stands or sits on a bar attached to a yoke between two bulls. The average time taken to complete the 100 metre course is about 9 seconds.

Martial Arts Indonesia's own fighting sport is known as 'Pencak Silat'. Competitors travel to Jakarta to take part in tournaments there.

Gazetteer

Official name: Republic of Indonesia

Constitution: Democratic Republic

Head of state: President of Indonesia (General Suharto, elected 1983)

Official language: Bahasa Indonesia

Area: Total land area covered by 13 677 islands and islets — 2 034 255 sq. km. Total area including territorial waters — 5 193 250 sq. km.

Population: 147 490 298

Average number of people per square kilometre: 73. The population density is greatest in Java where there are 681 people per square kilometre.

Highest mountain: Jayawijaya Mountain, 5500 m. It is in Irian Jaya.

Climate: Tropical monsoon with wet and dry seasons. Average temperatures vary with the place. Coastal areas average 27°C throughout the year. Inland areas average 25°C throughout the year. In the highlands there is snow all year on the highest peaks. Humidity is usually high.

Average annual rainfall: Jakarta — 1775 mm; Surabaya — 1285 mm.

Currency: The Rupiah (Rp) is divided into 100 sen

Weights and measures: The metric system has been used in Indonesia since 1923.

Main exports: Oil, coffee, rubber, vegetable oils, tin ore, tea, tobacco, copra, wood

Main imports: Special refined oils, rice, chemicals and fertilisers, iron and steel, industrial machinery

Main international airports: Jakarta, Bali (Denpasar)

Main shipping ports: Jakarta, Surabaya

Youth organisations: Scouts and guides

Membership of international organisations:
    United Nations
    Association of South East Asian Nations (ASEAN)
    The Non-Aligned Movement

The Indonesian National Anthem is 'Indonesia Raya', which means Indonesia The Great. It was composed in 1928. This is the first verse:

Indonesia, our native country
Our brithplace.
Where we all arise to stand guard
Over this our Motherland.
Indonesia our nationality,
Our people and our country
Come, let us all exclaim
Indonesia united.
Long live our land.
Long live our state.
Our nation, our people and all
Arouse the spirit and body
For Great Indonesia.

The Indonesian National Flag

The Indonesian Coat of Arms. The motto means 'Unity in Diversity' and was first used in the fifteenth century.

Index